The Park Bench

Sithanthi Alfred

BookLeaf Publishing

India | USA | UK

The Park Bench © 2024 Sithanthi Alfred

All rights reserved.

No part of this publication may be
reproduced, stored in a retrieval system, or
transmitted, in any form or by any means,
electronic, mechanical, photocopying,
recording or otherwise, without the prior
written permission of the presenters.

Sithanthi Alfred asserts the moral right to
be identified as the author of this work.

Presentation by *BookLeaf Publishing*

Web: www.bookleafpub.com

E-mail: info@bookleafpub.com

ISBN: 9789363310162

First edition 2024

To my father

ACKNOWLEDGEMENT

I thank heaven, my husband and my daughter for finally giving me the mind space and peace of mind to embark on this challenge. To help sustain the energy to produce a work of deep reflection and inspiration, I thank BookLeaf.

PREFACE

Poetry is indeed 'emotions recollected in tranquility' and must be expressed in a language 'simple' so that the 'common' people would read poetry. The 'Preface To The Lyrical Ballads' has partly been the cornerstone on which I have based my poems. But I differ with Wordsworth when he defines poetry as a 'passionate overflow of powerful feelings' because my experience with writing poetry has been an impassioned flow of ordinary feelings, taking some of the cues from T. S. Eliot's theory 'The Tradition and the Individual Talent'. I have also experimented with metaphysical poetry to some extent, mixing the concrete with the comet. The work has been divided into three parts, namely the Capricious Self, the Resonance, Women and Politics but the three parts overlap in theme, style and treatment.

Table of Contents

THE CAPRICIOUS SELF

The Journey of a lifetime

Ever heard anyone say
That they took
A train journey
As an excited, happy child
But on return briefly
She was a Tess of the D'Urberville
Burdened at the sight
Of yet another sibling
Her May Flower dance
Such a fleeting moment
Of ecstasy and pure joy
Her maidenhood mocked
Her magical metamorphosis slighted
Her colourful, patterned wings ridiculed
Her intelligent head laughed at
Her choice of friends and flowers frowned upon
Neither a fresh flower
Nor a winged butterfly
Maybe a dragonfly or a dirty flea
One could not be both
Beautiful and proud.

The Song

If it struck my eyes
Or blew my mind,
Or tugged at my heartstrings
Heartwarming images
On the walls, over the shelves
On the pages
I was the most blessed child
Chilling experiences
On the streets
And in the neighbourhood
I was the Devil's child
Once dug a hole to bury
a tiny sparrow dead
As a curious child wished
to see the bird escape
From a closed room, a ceiling fan on speed
Shocked at the unsuspecting bird drop dead
The bird slaughter
made me a grave digger
And a fugitive for life.

The School Bell

Never the morning bell
Always the evening knell
between school and home
The excitement and sheer happiness
lay in an enchanting park
luring children into a real school
Where teachers and books did not exist
But you were free to study what you liked
Watch the chameleon turn green
On the green grass
Then brown on the brown bark,
Red on the red croton plant
And grey on the grey stone path
Watch for the rainwater rising in the pond
Drowning the stone elephant calf
And the little wooden bridge
Watch out for the many coloured butterflies
Sometimes crush the pupa
To see the colours flow
Sometimes count the eggs in a bird's nest or
scare the bird-babies
Seamless joy in learning inside the park.

Do not paint the sheep black

Ever wondered
A black sheep
Has been black
Since inception
Born defiant
A sweet rebel
Yet the persecution
For being distinct
To appear disparate
To express divergent thoughts
In words or in silence
Dare or retreat
Any act passive or otherwise
Invites
The wrath
Of the herd
Why is it
A mammoth task
To rejoice at
The uniqueness?

The Smell of Sunday

Never could I recreate
Those Sundays of my childhood
Those were the times of plain soap
The odourless Lifebuoy soap
And the sandalwood-perfumed Mysore soap
Nothing special for the hair
maybe soapnut powder sometimes
Unforgettable was the vigorous dabbing
On the face with old cuticura powder, ponds
maybe.

Tennis on Colour TV

A fond memory
The new concept
Becoming a fangirl
Of tennis stars
Began with colour TV
Steffi Graf and Ivan Lendl.

My father and I
For a couple of years
The only time perhaps
We sat watching together
the quarter-finals, the semi-finals
And the finals of Wimbledon, French, Australian
and US Open.

Lendl regimented, a soldier, crazy serious
Every ball serving, every ball taken
Facial muscles stoned up, body frigid.
Ivan the Terminator
Dictated from the back of the court
With his powerful forehand
Why Wimbledon evaded him is a mystery
Was he paranoid about playing on clay?
He could not warm up, smile or release
the tension or so at Wimbledon!

Steffi was a ruthless forehand drive
on courts of all surfaces, deft footwork
But warmth, rare smiles for her fans
Her play style got the spectators
To dance to her magnificent shots.

Grandparents

Absent in my life
      Wonder if I might have had a different
personality
Happy, vivacious, confident
      Didn't folks complain that I was born
old? Wicked beyond years?
Discerning, critical, a prick
      Grandparents might have made my
good support system
Against overrated parental dispositions
      This smartass had to fend for herself
against entire family assault.

Eighties Love

Long distance
You might say
The dynamics of love
Even if one lived
On the opposite street
Love demanded patience
Like waiting
For a tortoise to cross the bridge called eternity
Plainly biding time and luck
For that moment
when each other's eyes locked
The pact writ in silence forever
Love unblemished, chaste
Only serotonin and dopamine
All the time
No touch, no lip lock
Yet constant
lovemaking of the minds
From across the street.

The Halley's Comet

The campus screamed
It was Footloose, Madonna and Maradona
At the college fest
Posters, T-shirts, music, dance ripped through
Madonna had peaked the girl's mania
For make-up, jive and jest
While the tomboys in Maradona hairdo
Zoomed around in Suzukis
They did kick footballs around on the basketball
court
Some of us had our head screwed over
Hamlet's 'to be or not to be'
I was procrastinating
To have a boyfriend or not to have a boyfriend
So much buzz went on about Halley
How the Comet would jet down from the skies
How your wishes might come true if you sight
 The Comet and instantly make your wish.
That's how I befriended a boy
 And married him too.

Relationships

No one really is
An open book
Stop believing
That you know someone
Remember they hurt you harder.

Some are cryptic puzzles
Nearly impossible to decipher
Terse in speech
Ambiguous in meaning
Mysterious in behaviour.

Some are jumbled, rumpled
In speech and action
Messy, mussy, muddled
Leave behind a trail
Of confusion and chaos.

Some are crossword puzzles
Appear neat, the lined boxes
Horizontal, vertical, diagonal
Here is where you find
The snitch, the sellout, the double cross.
Innocence and naivety are extinct
Good connections are time-bound
Not everlasting

Life is licking
One's own wounds everytime.

The Mask

Not easy this life without a mask
Each day, every single hour
The face needs a mask
Either people easily read your face
Or ignore the reading on the face
Better masked than exposed
The neediness, the vulnerabilities
The greediness, the evilness
I have fought most battles without a mask
I no longer battle but I need a mask now
To hide myself from my new self
The one that wishes no encounter
With friends or adversaries
Wear a mask and go incognito.

The Circus Dog

How many rings of fire
Have you leaped through?
Innumerable. Unscathed.
You are not in circus
You haven't been trained
It is what happens in life
Spectators love the circus
They never say
Stop! Enough of the cruelty! To the dog.
Dogs dread fire.
Does it have a choice?
For a karmic
It does not matter.
How many times she is put through
The wringer, she looks at it as a challenge,
Not forced labour!
Now please applaud!

Chaos

What you feel day long
Is a game of dart
Dodging the bullet or the bouncing ball
The heart paces, races, chases
There is never any quiet
I want to avoid them
Because I am not game
To their sinister plans
I wish to be friends with those others
They appear understanding
Maybe I will not get hurt
But I am not sure
I hope to explain myself
But I doubt if they have made up their mind
Their biases and prejudices
Their inherent dislike and unfairness
I rather remain misunderstood
Than fight to reveal the truth
Let my rivals and friends fight
with each other over my integrity
To hell with everybody!

Skittish over Sickness

If you ask me
What I am most scared of
It is me
What is within me
Not my mind and intellect
But inside of my body
Twitchy, antsy, nervy
Over viruses plotting
Over gangster cells scheming
Over foreign agents overstaying
When organs begin disobeying
angry and inflammatory
Sullen and shrinking
When the inside of you
Turns into a toxic playground
Upsetting and weakening
Old players, mocking and humiliating
Their loss of earlier resistance.

Gracias to AM for teaching me Gerard Manley Hopkins!

'The world is charged
    With the grandeur of God'
        Charged sounded so electric, so powered
           The shock shook and I was shaken
permanently!

It was not current infatuation
        Not a temporal energy attraction
          Hopkins had me insulated
            Against fluctuations and
crosswires.

His poems had free flowed into songs
    Within me like radio waves carrying
        Towards God's grandeur
          Like the chords to an instrument
strung.

A true poet floats through myriad spheres
    Darkness, delusions, pain and suffering
      And discovers light, en light in the end!
        Fear of life and death gone, love for
little things, everlast.

The Quest

Once upon a time in India
One's heart and mind
Would wander searching
For answers on who and what is god.

Did God have a form?
This God had many forms.
Male, female and half each side
Each form outdid the other.

The craftsmen were master craftsmen
Gods looked grander than kings and queens
The calendar Gods came alive each month.

In temples, the metal-crafted oil lamps lit up
The bells rang furiously sending your body into
freeze mode
For a moment, oh, here is your God
Who is that half-clothed man showing his back
And hiding the deity? Does he hold a monopoly
over the Gods?
Has anyone seen the deity without that man
standing in between?
No way, that God is his, cannot be yours?

That God in the village with her companions
The horse, the cow, the dog, the elephant
The little men who shepherd them
I could touch them, bathe them
Garland and seek their blessings
No one came in between.

In Search of Faith

I know
I am fulfilled
With the knowledge
Of the good and of God.

I spent
Looking for the supreme being
Outside of me
Yes in chapels, dargahs and temples.

Amazed at the mass faith outpouring
Such infallibility in their surrender
I envied them for their utter belief.

I had work to do, within me
I had to remove myself far away
Before I find my faith within me.

The Furniture

Two upright chairs
One teapoy and a square table
A small straight cot
The furniture over time
Acquired my father's personality
The rosewood was rock solid
Three generations are past
This small collection
My father's first possession
Has come to last long after he has passed
They do not make any statement
They stand still
Let generations walk past it.

The Park Bench

23

In the Cantonment in Bangalore
Inside the old Kensington park
Sitting on the old bench overlooking the lake
The same old bench on which my father sat
To study and make his career
Some seventy-odd years ago
As a twenty-something lad
Seeking fortune and fame and family
How fortunate for me!
That the park and bench exist
That's the ideal spot in mind
Where I mentally squat in comfort and write.

In Memory Of My Father

Life shone like the midday sun,
In one long summer of childhood.
Blooming like sunflowers full, in a little garden,
Down the street, sparkling broken trinkets
On the wayside strewn.
Magic unravelled all day, that summer.

In that one summer of sweet innocence,
Eagerly awaited the master storyteller.
He was the protagonist and all characters too.
He, His, Him. He was the story.
Home was the stage, the act, his alone.
The little man in there, the hero.
His little children, starstruck.

With kinsmen and clansmen,
Talking through the night,
Tales of ghosts and gods,
Rendezvous of the living and dead,
In the dead of sultry noon or eerie night.
From faraway lands and languages,
Stories, strange and sentimental,
Drinking from the deep well of memory,
Refreshed Kinsmen return separate ways.

The little man back on stage
Aware of much expectation
From his wide eyed, keen eared little audience
For performances, rare and real
That tormented, tested and teased
His young audience, and deeply touched.
A father's desire to leave imprints
On the sands of time.
His children curiouser.

One Evening in the Village

One evening
In my father's ancestral village
A place where
We had never stayed in
For lack of amenities
In our growing up years.

Many, many years later
I visited and stayed in
The evening was unforgettable
Never experienced anything like it
This was the closest I had been to nature.

The trees inside the hamlet resonated
To the hills baritone melodious.
The palms were absolute ballerinas
swaying in the gentle breeze
It touched me, evoking nostalgia.

I felt incredible that evening
At the memory of my father
Glad in the gladness for him
That I stayed in, that evening
And saw the song and dance
Of the hills and trees in his village.

Anniversary

He passed a decade ago
Yonder into a better world
Yet the heartbreak
Remains fresh, forlorn and fearful
As it was on that day
The pain still as excruciating as then
Everything as clear as in a mirror
Nothing forgotten, nothing absent
Time stood still. Time stands still.
Time does not heal.
Time is a great trickster.

The Story of a Home

To turn
A home
Into a tomb
Three decades
Is all it takes.

In time
The cracks appear on the walls
The mosaic chips the floors
The paint peels off the ceiling.

Flown off the nest, the noisy, quarrelsome birds
The elders free at last, they believe
The farthest the old birds fly
Was till the end of the road.

The Finish Line

29

I have scribbled aplenty
I worry if they will be read
I wonder if the reader will like them
I pray that some lines will be quotable
The thoughts and feelings expressed
Will leave the mind inspired and impressed.

I do not want to be in a logjam,
Where the cover of the book matters at all
Where the book description says it all
Where the author profile is eye-catching at all.

THE RESONANCE

Leaves of a Notebook

Walk leisurely
Into the God-made natural wonders
Than in uninspiring gardens
Made by man.

That one school excursion
To the verdant Western Ghats
Was the ultimate experience
Of God's own magical masterpiece.

The random pathway
Dead foliage, nettles and bramble
No pebbled paths, no stones laden
Just a jungle walkway.

Trees gigantic,
Shrubs, bushes jostling
Stunning hues of green
Up, down and every inch of the way
plants ostentatious.

Wildflowers in maddening colours
Ravishing reds, pretentious pinks, flamboyant
yellows
Wild berries shining,
Baffling blues, perplexing purples, flaming
orange.

No rules binding here
Touched the flowers, inhaled the fragrance,
Promptly plucked, to tuck
Between the leaves of a notebook.

Tasting the luscious berries, an instant sport
Sweet, sour, bitter, bland, salty, creamy whatnot
This nature walk, mystical, magical
The senses awakened to its fullest.

The Paper Boats

When you grow up in a city
With no seaside or a beach,
Not even a riverside or a riverbank.

When you are too young
To vividly imagine the illustrations
from the children's storybook.

The big oceans
The large boats
The giant ships.

The greatest joy
Emerges from the little paper boats.
They are set afloat in every small puddle
Where they rock gently,
And in the snake-like gutters
Where the rainwater rushes in rapidly,
The boats take off without a warning.

Delightful use of paper from a notebook
For the making of little paper boats
To fill up the puddles and the gutter
On rainy days after school.

Easter Morning

April
Summer in India
Half an hour past five o'clock
It is Easter morning
In Bangalore.
We are approaching
The Philharmonic Street
Lined up on both sides
Large evergreen deciduous old trees
They stage the world's rare concert
In the middle of the city.
The violin, the mandolin. The flute, the
harmonium.
Every known Indian bird gathered in the trees
They pitched, popped, piped symphonious
The promenade pulsated, the note, the number
The goldfinches chirped infinite notes
The wrens trilled, the sparrows chiddiked
The raucous crows cawed at regular intervals
The nightingales sang softly
Accompanied by buzzing black-chinned
hummingbirds
The Philharmonic Street, a giant hammock
Swinging between heaven and earth
The music crescendoed
And the mortals transcended

For the humans flaunting
Their plumes inside the church
Folks had missed the heavenly interlude
Easter was the day to feel heaven on earth
Bird songs are God's own choir
What best way to celebrate revival,
Of hope, of faith and fortitude
At the Philharmonic Street.

The Louvre

On a recent trip to Europe
Though we checked on Google
The vastness and intricate accesses
Into the famous Louvre
Yet were we so unprepared
For the drama unravelling soon.

My daughter asked us to take the elevator
She would walk up the stairs and join us
The meeting did not take place.

We paced up and down many floors
Silently cursing French art
So much red and carnations in their paintings.

The colours were upping my blood pressure
I wished to see landscapes in calmer colours
And find my daughter.

Took the elevator up and down and up.
Hundreds moving from one section to another.
We stood in the hall showcasing the Mona Lisa
Because she definitely wanted to see this.

No sign of her! No phone signals!
Didn't know how deep down or high up we were
Louvre was a cosmos, we were not astronauts.

Tried hard to retrace our steps from where we
started
We could not get there.
We got into the elevator on one side
And got out from the other side
My daughter remained where she left us
On the other side of the cosmos.

Pacing up and down different floors
Taking the elevator up and down and up
All she wanted was to see were her parents
Cursing the French pale white bold sculptures
Of naked men and women
Curled hair, long legs, torsos, chests and breasts
Sometimes noticing mother and child
Or Jesus Christ and his apostles
Helped her calm down.

The one hope left was to leave the cosmos
Get out and connect soon
Visiting Rembrandt's house was easy
Like climbing the tree to see his tree house.

The Drive

Remember an old poem
About a bicycle
Rode by a boy
Up the hill and down the hill
In maddening joy and exhilaration?
This was not a hill!
It was the Western Ghats
Driving uphill can be a task
Navigating traffic can be an uphill task.
Rarely do accidents occur though,
When you are on the way to Goa.
Looking out the window
Will not cause you vertigo
Your destination is all
That is on your mind.
One has never had enough of Goa,
But one must return
Unless you are a lotus eater.
Be warned though
The road down via Amboli to your destination
Is where and when you will develop vertigo
Not merely vertigo, you will be delirious
And speak in strange languages.
The fear is stuck in your throat.
You cannot articulate.
To be driving down

From two thousand feet above sea level
Unable to block one's eyes
from the bottom scene
Which was green and more green
And my favourite place to be in.
This one time I prayed
To be excused
Because I had miles to go
Before calling it quit
To my tryst with life on earth.
The road being narrow
The seat on either side could not help
Hide the view or the panic
In my frozen look and stiffened body.
Two hours of hell of a drive
Uphill to paradise, downhill through hell
and back to daily life.

Death

High Tide
Magnificent moon
Cast through the palm trees
Dreamy light on the shore
Over some shanty palm huts strewn on the sand.

On a beach chair anxiously waiting
To watch the ocean rise and enter
And reach as they said a marked boundary
A little beyond where I sat.

High tide anywhere else
Coastguards shooed you home
But here in Havelock Beach in Andamans
Barring a few white tourists in blissful stupor
It was remote, out of reach.

The small stretch of the heavenly island
Fell under the intense, inimical gaze of the moon
The waters treacherous at the word go
Menacing, malevolent, maniacal surge
I was raring to watch the ocean reach me.

Got my eyes fixated on a piece of black wood
Brought in by the ocean
I began to think it was a black dog
That needed to be chased away
Before being carried away by the ocean.

Momentarily delirious, nearly hallucinating
Looking at the surging water
A sudden urge to walk towards and into it
Took hold of me for a second, suicidal in a flash!

More shocking was a mysterious
Unknown feeling of joy deep inside,
A certain fear of death
Had vanished in that moment.

The Fury

Decades of sparse rain
Naturally dried-up rivers and wells
A city with the longest coastline
Yet here was a ship run out of water
Rain was the only answer
Then it poured one day
It poured and poured and poured a lot more
The Adyar River had been condemned
She was a barren old unbearable hag
Who would have thought
A river past menopause
Suddenly have a swollen stomach
Pregnant with disaster
A city under threat
Then the water broke
And quietly flowed on the streets
Steadily and dangerously rising and rising
Filling the basements and falling into the deep
long dried up wells
Largely a stealth attack from the river
You could not hear it passing through the streets,
filling up the basements
Only the waterfall into the neighbour's well.

The electricity shut down. No mobiles, no
computers, no ferries.
Aircrafts dropping food on the terraces.
We had no such luck.
Just waited for her to calm down.

A Cyclone in 1978

From the veranda of the seaside bungalow
one afternoon, an intense convergence
Of dark clouds overcast
The Arabian Sea swirled, swished, seethed
Into a hungry, shape-shifting black giant
The sky angrily drew a dark, black canopy,
As rain slapped hard from underneath.
The mountains and islands stood testimony
To a terrifying demonic dance
The atmosphere dense, the drama damning
The storm a virtual horror unfolding
The black magic condensed in a giant bottle
One just looked at it with naked eyes
Not as caught on camera today,
The sea's reclamation of land.

The Dog World

I am not a mean bitch
It's just that I had my nose in books
Rather than the dogs outside
I didn't become a dog person until
My child was born and became my teacher
For studies on dog humanity
And human evolution.
At ten years, watched a great-looking street dog
Ramu
Receive public honour at his burial
Haven't seen any such for humans yet
The memory had been buried deep in my psyche
Maybe I am a callous bitch
I let a healthy dog fall sick and die
I had struck a rapport with him
Eye contact isn't enough I guess
You need to take care
The next one lived long
But it's not how long but how well
One has lived that matters
I saw him as a servant, a watchdog
Put his food on the floor, no bowl for him
I beat myself up everyday
For having been a mean bitch
The next one commanded nothing
But unconditional respect and service

I was wired to his needs
His looks and barks
Would set off little alarms in my brain
I was His Majesty's full-time servant.

Little Ulysses

Scrawny
Scraggly
Limp
Bony
Sick!
His last bark
As sharp
As the first one.
This time
He barked,
With the same vigour.
Summoned us,
To curtly
Bid us
Goodbye.
Once long ago
Little Ulysses's
Lush long black
Shiny hair
Fell to the floor
Like a velvety black robe
Distinguished
Him highly
And like Ulysses,
Become a name
and a part of all that he met.

The City Doomed

After most of the world
with its people
is wiped out
By nuclear war
And natural calamities
The survivors
will unite and reject
The ideas of their predecessors,
the old order.

The concept of city
as a symbol
of civilizational progress
Will be debunked,
the concrete done away with.
the soil, slush sand, stone once again
To rebuild the old way of life.

City Unrecognisable!

City unrecognisable!
Lived your entire life here
But the city neither is recognisable
Nor does it recognise me.

Where did the trees and lakes go
About them, we had prided so
People from elsewhere moved here
For its splendid weather alone.

All I see is a concrete wonder world
The flyovers and metros running overhead
The dark, dirty narrow service roads beneath
Are cities only for motorways and metro trains
Is that a measure of progress for the
Government?

Time Is Static

Anybody notice
The time
during which
The action
Takes place
In your dream?

It is never
A sunny day
Nor a rainy day
Always a dull day
A black and white film
Time is static
In inertia the action.

Faded, sad, ominous
Ancestors come and go
Warning of dangers
Lurking below
Sometimes foretelling
Fortunate events
To manifest somehow.

WOMEN AND POLITICS

I See a Woman

I see a woman
As a wondrous horse, not a warm cow
Do not squeeze
The idea of a woman to a wet nurse.
Feminine is not bovine
What is wrong with you!
She is much more
Before and after
She turns a mother
Watch the races she runs
A nimble mare to a marvel
Not merely an astonishing beauty
Look at the impregnability
Resistance and robustness
Look how she precipitates
Coasts, glissades, soars and wings
Streams, flows, rolls, runs.
She gives it all
For the sport called life
For the sheer joy of the spectators
Right until her strength wanes
Sometimes asking herself
Why did she not choose
To trot mindfully over the meadows
instead of racing blindly on the course.

Rest in Peace

53

Standing atop a green hill in the Nilgiris
A quaint old church
Hides an interesting piece of cemetery behind
Every single headstone
Of white men and women
Has stood the test of time
Honoured, immortalised

Rest in peace is white, privileged,
Grand is the Christian burial
In his own country or in the colony
The natives get a single pillar
At the village square
Engraved on it is 'to the unknown'

Elsewhere in a nearby city
In the twenty-first century
Grave diggers cease to dig six feet
No time to decompose in peace
Old bodies dug up, new bodies laid in
Christian burial signals 'rest briefly'.

Marriage Woes

A marriage lacks sorely
the solemnity
  And wisdom in the sacrament
Exchanged at the ceremony.

Even from the priest,
    parents, families, the community.
No one is present or mindful, the bride and
groom too.
    Storm brews on the eve,
Of the wedding, the reception even the
honeymoon
    And the rest of your new life,
 until you begin to hate it.

Happiness and other honeymoon fantasies end
swiftly
    People cannot bear
the idea of a new couple wasting time.
    There's the routine
imposed, chores allotted
    The employee with the shortest of
probation
She falls short in everything
    No suspension, no dismissal,

a long period of lament by in-laws
        Heard by the family,
the girl's family, the neighbourhood
        Every friend or relative
who comes through that door
        Didn't they promise to see her as their
own daughter?

Spring is gone, summer arrives, offspring too
some distance and quiet from the chaos
a deep immerse, a frog in the well period
a long period of isolation
Until you forget who you were and what you
wanted in life.

The monsoon has come.
The rains wash away delusions
The crazy ideas of how we would live and grow
old together
Had been bombed at the altar
With due respect to Shakespeare
Indian marriages are between and among several
true minds
They admit impediments, alter frequently until
the edge of doom.

From dawn to dusk

It's great
people waking up
to worship the sun god.
It's amazing even more
Farmers waking up hours early
To prepare for the worship
Of the creatures at home.

The cocks crowed after her
The cows mooed soon after
The sheep sheepishly bleated
The pigs sleepily grunted
The ducks struggled
To get the ducklings in a row.

It is clockwork for the farmer
The fields are calling
But her animals and birds need feeding before
No time to wait for the sun god to rise.

Shaheen Bagh

The protest
will go down
In History
As one
which electrified
the nation.
Jerked the people
out of their slumber
Shook them out of fear
of the state.
The police state
was looked straight at
in the face
By the women
at Shaheen Bagh
And they roared
Hum kagaz nahi dikhayenge
We will not show the papers
We are citizens of this nation!

In the likeness of me

Hey son,
Do not look,
For a girl,
Made in the likeness of me,
Your mother. That's delusion,
That is a lie.

Me and You,
Lived life as in, an amusement park.
I let you ride, all the rides.
I let you eat, all the eats.
I let you swig, slurp and smack.
You rocked the horse
Till it could spring no more.
You wheeled until giddy with sheer joy,
The tiniest of merry go round
To the giant round carousel.
Time to get out and get a life, son!

Come back here,
When the silver streak shows,
When your body looks for the recliner,
When I am no more around,
When watching life around is joy enough.
Until then, say goodbye to me!

Hey son,
Look for a girl,
That is unlike me.
Whose dreams are alive,
Not buried in the base of your home.

Find a girl unlike me,
Raring, for the take-off,
Like a Falcon or a Pelican,
Flying over oceans and continents,
To chill over peaks untouched by man.
Let her be the pilot and you the co-pilot.
Caress her wings, kiss her restless eyes,
Lounge with her on the mountain cliff,
See the sky and the sea fuse serenely,
In the not-so-far horizon.

Do not live,
In the madness of the times,
Do not let them stuff you in a box,
And call you sons of God or War
Or call you daughters of fortune or destiny
Or some such ludicrous phrase.
Spread your wings and take the plunge,
The bungee jumping of a life.
Breathe in the fantastic freedom,
And live as crazy poets or kings do.

Hey son,
Look for a girl,
That is unlike me.
Whose dreams are alive,
Not buried in the base of her home.

The Assassination of Indira

The newspapers, an overload!
Khalistanis holed up inside the Golden Temple.
The army directed to flush them out.
Pakistan avenging the birth of Bangladesh.
Another partition in the throes of birthing.
The Prime Minister dealt with an iron hand.
Crushed the Cause for Khalistan.
She had to pay with her life.

India, one nation, one national TV.
The whole nation watched
The news of the assassination.
News trickled like drops of water
From a broken tap.
Didn't know if she had died or not.
The Editor was on a leash.
Salma Sultan, the deadpan faced newsreader,
Let two tear drops cascade down her stony face.
She was yet to be permitted
To announce the news,
But the nation knew, just from her teardrops.

Slaining Truth

62

Why does a woman wielding a pen
Cause such terrifying fear among powerful men?
How does a pen send a ripple down the spine of
the muscled and moneyed men?
Does a pen bring down Governments?
Does a pen really kill?
Fame and fortune of men?

A pen that dares to speak truth to power
A pen that questions the power equation
Her intuition was solidly bang on!
And she began to fire away like a machine gun
targeting the new powers that be, with her pen
The assassins hired by cowardly mastermind
Coldly shot her from the dark shadows
Of her own home.

Political

Yes, political!
From cradle to the grave.
Yet men do not agree
That women could be political
Astute, judicious, fair.
No woman worth her salt
Could run her home
Without the political acumen.
She is a political warrior.
No sword fighting, fencing or boxing.
Just a sharp mind
Even sharper tongue.
Everything wrong in the home
And in the world
Could be set right by women alone.
Remember Sojourner Truth's words
'If the world is upside down
The women will turn it right side up!'

The Period

The cotton-filled, quiet blue skies,
Steadily took on fearful hues of black,
Soon hell bawled blasts of deadly winds,
To power obliteration and annihilation around.

Tall trees transfixed one moment,
Twisted and felled the next.
Coconut fronds flew like paper planes
Before crashing among mounds of leaves
Mighty branches mercilessly break down.

In the deep of consciousness, rage soared
Even as rains lashed and beat society
Of complacency, cowardice and coldness
The time had come to clip the little bird's wings.

The tempestuous storm had breached.
The hormones unleashed.
The vagina pained and shaken, bloodied.
Silent sorrow and loud angry voices in the head.
Unabashedly smirching the skirt in public.
The period. The shame.
In the deep of consciousness.

The Migrant Labourer

The migrant trudges
along the highway
He cares not to look
behind at the concrete jungle
a jungle whose heart was a mere pile of stones
Its soul, merely a sack of sand
a jungle inside which
he left his handprints, footprints, sweat and spit
he is caught between the Devil
and the deep unknown
he knows not what awaits him
Is he walking straight into the arms of Death
Is he going in circles to die of exhaustion
he is no longer needed, that he knows.

Middle Class Maladies

Be a failure
Families shun you
Tease and test you
You will be a punching bag
And funnily their comfort pillow
When they hit a low.

Be a success
Families stun you
Suspect and scorn you
You will be their punching bag
And scarily their object of ridicule
When they reek of jealousy.

Be silent about everything
They will wait a while
Suspect and slander you
You will be their crime story
And a serious case to solve
Then hastily come storming to your door.

The Cantonment Sports Scene

The time before TV arrived
The country held the transistor to its ears
To listen to cricket commentaries.

Girls moved from skipping to basketball
football and volleyball
they bravely wore shorts to the playground
sportswomanship was the hallmark of liberation.

That one time, and for the first time
Watched live, female football pros
Pitched for a match
At East Railway Station grounds
Being one of few female spectators
I sat glued, transformed and transcended.

This one match changed me about
What women can do
Tackle, pass, pass back, dribble, kick, kick-off
Centre, forward, dummy, attack
Beautiful, strong players, all eyes on that ball!
Not a bunch of giggling girls
Trying to catch the eyes of road Romeos.

www.ingramcontent.com/pod-product-compliance
Lightning Source LLC
La Vergne TN
LVHW011054200726
843509LV00011B/1406

*9 7 8 9 3 6 3 3 1 0 1 6 2 *